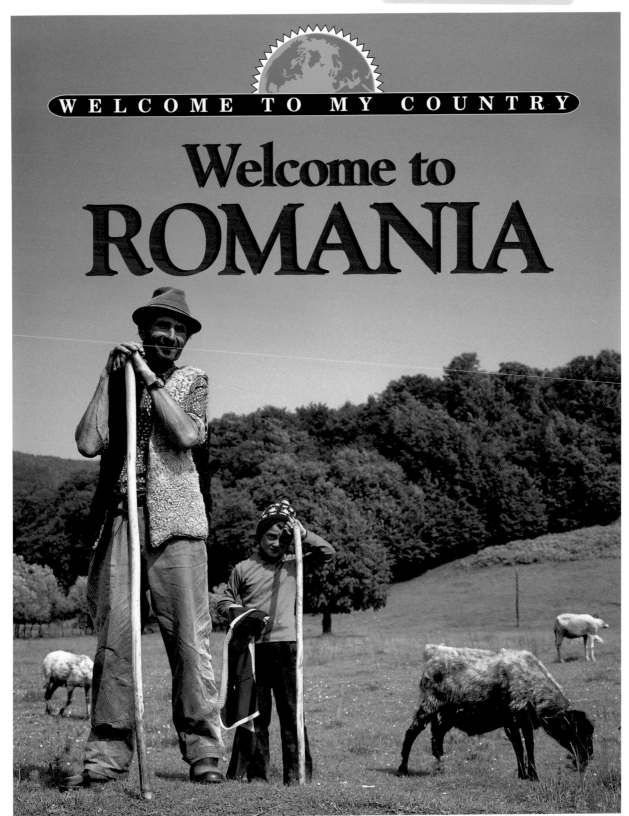

WELCOME TO MY COUNTRY

Welcome to
ROMANIA

FRANKLIN WATTS
LONDON · SYDNEY

PICTURE CREDITS
Art Directors & TRIP Photographic Library:
cover, 1, 2, 3 (centre and bottom), 7, 8,
20 (bottom), 21, 25, 28, 31, 33, 35, 38,
39, 40, 43, 45
Michele Burgess: 3 (top), 4, 13, 16, 26, 32
Jan Butchofsky /Houserstock: 6, 27 (bottom)
Camera Press: 23
Focus Team – Italy: 9, 27 (top), 41
Getty Images/Hulton Archive: 15 (top and
bottom), 36
Bridget Gubbins: 20 (top)
Haga Library, Japan: 22
Sonia Halliday Photographs: 5
Dave G. Houser/Houserstock.: 18, 19
The Hutchison Library: 29
North Wind Picture Archives: 10, 11, 12
Pankotay/Camera Press: 17
David Rubinger/Camera Press: 14
Karen Stow/Camera Press: 30 (top)
Liba Taylor: 24
Travel Ink: 30 (bottom), 34
Bill Vetell/Camera Press: 37

Digital Scanning by Superskill Graphics Pte Ltd

This edition first published in 2005 by
Franklin Watts
96 Leonard Street
London EC2A 4XD

Franklin Watts Australia
45-51 Huntley Street
Alexandria NSW 2015

This edition is published for sale only in the United Kingdom & Eire.

© Marshall Cavendish International (Asia) Pte Ltd 2005
Originated and designed by Times Editions–Marshall Cavendish
an imprint of Marshall Cavendish International (Asia) Pte Ltd
A member of the Times Publishing Group
Times Centre, 1 New Industrial Road
Singapore 536196

Written by: Grace Pundyk
Editor: Melvin Neo
Designer: Geoslyn Lim
Picture researcher: Susan Jane Manuel

A CIP catalogue record for this book
is available from the British Library.

ISBN 0 7496 6013 9

Printed in Singapore

Contents

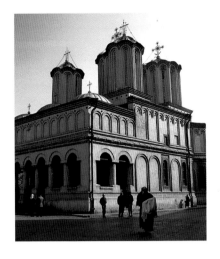

Words that appear in the glossary are printed in **boldface** type the first time they occur in the text.

Welcome to Romania!

Romania is located in southeastern Europe. The country is a beautiful land of rivers, lakes, mountains and plains. Romania is rich in cultural traditions which Romanians have fought to keep during centuries of war and **invasions**. Let's explore stunning Romania and learn about its interesting people!

Opposite: At the end of this street in Bucharest sits the huge Palace of Parliament. It is one of the world's largest buildings.

Below: Many men and women in Romania work on farms. Farming is one of the country's largest industries.

The Flag of Romania

Romania's flag is divided into three sections of blue, yellow and red. While the origin of the flag's colours is uncertain, some believe they were part of flags raised during battles against the invading Ottoman Turks and Hungarians.

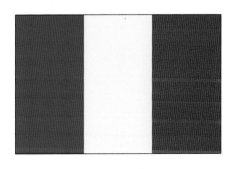

The Land

Romania's land area is 237,500 square kilometres. It is surrounded by five countries: Hungary, Ukraine, Moldova, Serbia and Montenegro, and Bulgaria. To the east, the Black Sea creates about 225 kilometres of coastline. The Black Sea coast, which lies at sea level, is Romania's lowest point. The highest point in Romania is Mount Moldoveanu. It stands 2,544 metres high.

Left: The Black Sea is a favourite summer vacation spot for many Romanians. These people enjoy a visit to the beach in Dobruja, a region in the southeastern part of Romania.

Mount Moldoveanu is located in the Transylvanian Alps, which form part of the Carpathian Mountain Range. Hills, **plateaus** and plains make up a large part of Romania's land. They are dotted with over 2,300 lakes. Lake Razelm, the country's largest lake, covers 415 square kilometres. Romania's largest river, the Danube River, flows along Romania's southern border for about 1,075 kilometres before emptying into the Black Sea.

Above:
This man is rowing his boat through the calm waters of the Danube Delta, which is the region where the Danube River empties into the Black Sea.

Climate

Romania has four different seasons. Summers are mostly sunny with many rain showers and some thunderstorms. Winters are cloudy, cold and snowy. In Bucharest, Romania's capital city, temperatures can reach 30° Celsius in summer and drop to -7° C in winter. The rainiest months in Romania are from April to June and from September to October. The country gets an average of 635 millimetres of rain each year. Twice as much rain falls in the mountains as on the plains.

Plants and Animals

Forests cover about 25 per cent of the country's land, including Romania's mountain regions, where trees such as beech, oak, pine and spruce grow.

Animals such as red deer, brown bears and lynx live in Romania. Rare antelopes called chamois live in high regions of the Carpathian Mountains. The Black Sea and the country's many rivers and lakes are also rich in animal life, including salmon, herring and eels.

Below: Many types of birds live in the Danube Delta area, which is located on the northern edge of Romania's Black Sea coastline.

History

In about 2000 B.C., groups of people called the Thracians moved to what is now Romania. The Greeks moved into the region in the seventh century B.C. They called the Thracians the Getae. The Romans **conquered** the region, which they called Dacia, in A.D. 106. They ruled Dacia until A.D. 271. Over the next eight hundred years, several groups conquered Dacia. One of these groups, the Slavs, settled in the region. Over the years, the Slavs and Dacians combined into one **ethnic** group. They were the early **ancestors** of Romanians.

Below:
Under Roman rule, many government officials, soldiers and traders came to Dacia. They changed Dacia's government and brought a new language, Latin. They also built many new cities.

From Hungarians to Ottoman Turks

By the early eleventh century A.D., the Hungarians had invaded. They claimed parts of Transylvania. To escape them, many Dacians moved south or east. By 1359, the Dacians had formed two separate **principalities** called Walachia and Moldavia. In the 1400s, invading Ottoman Turks took over but allowed the principalities to rule themselves. In the 1700s, the Turks took total control. The Turks often ruled dishonestly and harshly, causing many people to suffer.

Russian Rule and Independence

During the 1700s, the people of what is now Romania, especially the Orthodox Christians, were treated very poorly. In 1774, the Russians promised to protect the Orthodox Christians. In return, the Christians supported Russia in its fight against the Ottomans. By 1829, the Russians controlled Walachia and Moldavia. The Russians later lost power. In 1859, Alexandru Cuza was elected the ruler of both Moldavia and Walachia. The two lands later joined to form one nation, Romania. In 1878, Romania gained formal independence.

Left: This drawing depicts Bucharest when it was the capital of Walachia (1659–1862). In 1862, under ruler Alexandru Cuza, Bucharest became the capital of the nation of Romania.

The Two World Wars

In 1916, Romania joined World War I and fought on the side of the Allies, which included Russia, Britain, France and the United States. The Allies fought against Austria-Hungary and Germany. After the war Romania gained several large pieces of land. It later lost most of those regions. In 1939, World War II began. The country fought on the side of Germany. After the Soviet Union invaded Bucharest, Romania switched sides and declared war on the Germans.

Above: The Arch of Triumph, located in Bucharest, was built to honour Romania's World War I victory over Germany and Austria-Hungary.

Left: Nicolae and Elena Ceauşescu were found guilty of causing the deaths of about sixty thousand Romanians. They had told soldiers to fire into crowds of angry citizens gathered in a city square. They were both put to death on 25 December 1989.

The Communist Years and Beyond

After World War II, Romania became a **communist** nation. It was renamed the People's Republic of Romania in 1947. In 1965, Nicolae Ceauşescu became the leader of Romania. He ruled harshly and used special police forces to take control of all political, economic and social life in Romania. In 1989, he was taken from power after large **uprisings** broke out nationwide. Ion Iliescu was elected president in 1990. Romania has been a **democratic** nation ever since.

Stephen the Great (1435–1504)

Throughout his reign, Stephen the Great defended Romania against invasions by the Ottoman Turks, the Hungarians and the Poles. Because he worked to defend Christianity and the Romanian people, he was called the "Athlete of Christ".

King Carol I

Michael the Brave (1558–1601)

Michael the Brave, prince of Walachia, conquered Transylvania and Moldavia. He was the first to unite the three lands that would become modern Romania.

King Carol I (1839–1914)

King Carol I led Romania to gain its independence from the Ottoman Turks in the War of Independence (1877–1878).

Queen Marie

Queen Marie (1875–1938)

Famous for her charm and intelligence, Queen Marie was a great supporter of the arts. After World War I, she helped to **negotiate** Romania's gain of lands.

Government and the Economy

Romania is now a democratic **republic**. The Romanian government is made up of three main branches. The executive branch, led by the president, consists of a prime minister and the Council of Ministers. The ministers serve as advisors to the president. Parliament, or the legislative branch, is divided into the Senate and the Chamber of Deputies. The judicial branch is made up of the Supreme Court of Justice and county, local and military courts.

Below:
This grand building is the Palace of Parliament. It is where Romania's parliament meets. The building was known as the House of the People when the country was a communist nation.

Local Government and the Military

Romania is divided into forty-two regions. Forty-one of the regions are counties, which are called *judete*. The last region, Bucharest, is a **municipality**. All of the forty-two regions have their own independent, local governments. Each region is led by a *prefect*.

In Romania, all men must serve in the military. They join when they turn twenty years old. Most of them serve between twelve and eighteen months.

Above: Many tanks were brought in by Nicolae Ceauşescu to control the large anti-government uprisings of 1989. Instead, the soldiers turned against the ruler and helped the citizens bring down Ceauşescu's government.

The Economy

The Romanian economy has struggled since the fall of communism. Money from the International Monetary Fund (IMF) allowed Romania to make steps toward a strong economy. These steps included paying money owed to other nations and **privatising** industries. The government is also trying to control the cost of services and goods in Romania, but prices keep rising. Since 2000, the poverty level has started to decline but in 2002, 28.9 per cent of the people in Romania still lived in poverty.

Above: Romania ships most of its **exports** to Italy, Germany and France. Romania buys most of its goods from those same countries.

Farming and Other Industries

Wheat, maize, sugar beets, potatoes and grapes are the main crops in Romania. Fish and caviar, or fish eggs, are other important products. Romania produces cement, machinery and chemicals. It also produces iron, steel and wood products. Romania used to produce oil, but it has been used up. Today, mining products include coal, iron, copper and lead. Since the fall of communism, the tourism industry has become important.

Below: The growing of grapes and the making of wine are important industries in Romania. These vines are part of the Murfatlar vineyards in Dobruja which are among the best in the country.

People and Lifestyle

Romania's population is made up of many ethnic groups. The largest group is the ethnic Romanians. Others include Roma, who originally came from India, Hungarians, Ukrainians and Germans. Small numbers of Serbs, Croats, Turks, Russians, Tatars and other groups also live in the country. The government has officially accepted eighteen of the small ethnic groups in Romania. Each has a seat in the country's parliament.

Above: These ethnic Hungarian boys from Szek, or Sic, a village in Transylvania, are wearing traditional costumes.

Left: A girl and boy pose in a snow-covered mountain region of Romania. Women in Romania often outlive men. The women live an average of seventy-four years, while men average only sixty-seven years.

From the Countryside to the City

People in **rural** Romania have strong traditions and religious values. Their lifestyles are very different from those living in **urban** areas. Many rural Romanians refuse to own modern equipment, such as washing machines and refrigerators. They prefer to use traditional methods of washing clothes and preserving food. Strict rules also control how rural men and women meet. In Romania's cities, most lifestyles are much more modern.

Above: Boys in a rural region of Romania pose with their homemade wooden carts. About 45 per cent of Romanians live in rural areas. The other 55 per cent live in cities, such as Bucharest, Iaşi or Constanţa.

Family Life

Romanian families are generally very close. In the past, it was common for married children and their parents to live together. Today, many newlywed couples live in their own homes. It is still common for elderly Romanians to live with their grown children, who care for them. In Romania, having children is considered important. During the rule of Ceauşescu, married women had to have at least five children. Today, most women have just two children.

Below: Romanian newlyweds pose in traditional wedding outfits. Romanians in the cities usually get married later in life than those in the countryside.

Left: Not all children in Romania have families or homes. Many children live in orphanages or on the streets. They are sometimes called "Ceauşescu's children," because Ceauşescu was the one who ordered Romanian families to have five or more children even if the parents could not afford to raise them.

Women in Romania

In Romania, women make up about half of the **workforce**. In the cities, women usually work in the health, education and manufacturing fields. In rural areas, most women work on farms. Romania's government has passed laws to improve working conditions for women. Women are now serving in parliament as well. Even with these changes, most women are still treated unequally and often earn less than men for doing the same job.

Education

Romanian children between ages seven and fourteen must attend school. The first four years are called elementary school. The next four years are called lower secondary school. After students complete lower secondary school, they can choose to attend secondary school. Romania has five different types of secondary schools, including general education, teacher-training, **vocational**, art and physical education schools.

Below:
In many areas of Romania, the main language spoken is not Romanian. The students in those areas are usually taught in their own languages which include Hungarian and German.

Higher Education

Romania has many public and private universities. These schools are often expensive. The government gives some students in public universities money to help with costs. Most study programmes last for four to six years, depending on the course of study. Popular courses include medicine, law, economics and political science. Many students enjoy taking part in programmes that allow them to study in other countries for a time.

Above:
The University of Bucharest is the oldest university in Romania. It was built in 1694.

Religion

More than 80 per cent of the Romanian people are Christians. There are many different groups of Christians however, including Orthodox Christian, Catholic and Protestant groups. About 70 per cent of the people belong to the Romanian Orthodox Church. About 6 per cent are Catholics who belong to either Uniate or Roman Catholic churches. Another 6 per cent of Romanians are Protestant.

Above:
The Patriarchal Cathedral in the city of Bucharest was built in the 1600s. Prince Carol, who became Romania's King Carol I, and his wife Elizabeth were crowned king and queen in the cathedral in 1881.

Other Christian groups in Romania include Presbyterians, Pentecostalists, Baptists and Jehovah's Witnesses.

Most of the remaining 18 per cent of Romanians do not belong to a religion. A small number are followers of the religion of Islam. Many Jewish people used to live in Romania, but most have moved to other countries. Some people are members of the *Căluşari*, a religious group that dates back hundreds of years. Most of their traditions and practices are kept secret.

Above:
This **mosque** is located in the town of Constanţa. The 1991 **constitution** gave all Romanians the right to freely practise their own religious beliefs.

Left: A nun sells religious items at a shop in the Voroneţ convent, which is a house for nuns. Stephen the Great built the convent in the 1400s.

Language

The official language of Romania is Romanian. Romanian is also called Daco-Romanian. It is a Romance language, meaning it came from the Latin language. Spanish, Italian and French are also Romance languages. Romanian is very different from those languages because Romania is located close to Hungary and to countries that speak Slavic languages. Romania now uses some Hungarian and Slavic words as well as words taken from the Turks.

Left: This building is the Romanian Academy. It was founded in 1866 and is an important centre of research. More than seven million publications are housed in the academy's library.

Literature

In the late 1600s, many great works of literature were published in Romania. Most of them were religious works or books of poetry.

In the 1800s, Grigore Alexandrescu became well known for his **satires** and **fables**. Mihail Eminescu is recognised for creating modern Romanian poetry. Romanian play writer Eugène Ionesco was one of the most famous authors of the twentieth century. Ionesco's works led to a new theatre performance style.

Arts

Religious Architecture

Romania's religious buildings are an important part of the country's history. In Moldavia, there are many beautiful **monasteries**. Many of them were built in the 1400s and 1500s and have fancy, painted decorations on the inside and outside walls. Walachia's monasteries are known for their rich decorations. They date mostly from the 1500s and 1600s. Many buildings in Transylvania were created in the **Baroque** style.

Above: Moldavian monasteries of northern Romania are painted both inside and outside with detailed religious paintings.

Left: The Three Hierarchs Church, located in Iași, was built in the seventeenth century.

Romanian Theatre

Romanians love going to the theatre. Some experts believe that theatre in Romania dates back to the time of the Dacians. It was only after the Oravita Theatre was built in 1817, however, that going to the theatre became very popular. In a short time, many other theatres were built all over Romania. By the 1980s, nearly seven million Romanians were attending plays. By 1996, Romania had fifty-two theatres.

Above: Built in 1953, the National Opera House in Bucharest can hold about one thousand people.

Folk Songs and Music

Singing and dancing in Romania are important in both everyday life and at major events. Romanians sing or dance during events such as weddings, funerals and religious ceremonies. Village women sing together during and after their work. Romanians also play music on instruments such as a violin; a *cobză*, a stringed instrument; or a *țambal*, an instrument played like a xylophone.

Above: Romanian folk dances are colourful and lively. They are performed for entertainment and for religious ceremonies. The dances date back to many periods in history and have different styles of music and different dance steps.

Romanian Crafts

Romania is famous for its many crafts, including wooden and stone carvings, pottery, **embroidered** costumes and handwoven carpets. Many Romanians make a living by selling crafts made at home or in village workshops. Men are usually the potters and carvers. Women usually do the sewing and weaving. The beautiful, embroidered costumes made by rural Romanian women often sell for lots of money in many other countries.

Below: Many rural Romanian women still own hand-operated looms, which they use to make colourful carpets and rugs.

Leisure

Most Romanians work very hard, but they also like to have fun. Families in Romania often take summer vacations near the Black Sea or in the Carpathian Mountains. Some people go camping, swimming or fishing. Romanians in rural areas often house tourists on their land. Many city people enjoy staying in rural lodges to relax and enjoy nature. Romania also has many hot springs and **mineral springs**. Thousands of tourists from Romania and from other countries enjoy bathing in the springs each year.

Left: These men in Braşov are playing a game of chess. Playing chess is a popular leisure activity in Romania.

At home, many Romanians enjoy chatting over meals and spending time with family members. They also enjoy playing chess and card games such as rummy. Many people also attend art festivals or cultural events. Visiting museums and going to opera or theatre performances are popular leisure activities for those who can afford it. Wealthier Romanians may also play golf or tennis, dine in restaurants, go to movies or dance in nightclubs.

Above: Skiing in winter and rock climbing and hiking in summer are just a few of the sports Romanians enjoy when they visit the mountains. Many Romanians also love to visit the mountains to enjoy fresh air and nature.

Soccer in Romania

Soccer is by far Romania's favourite sport. Romanians love to play soccer. They also love to watch soccer games. In 1994, the Romanian team became famous for reaching the quarterfinals of the World Cup soccer championship, which was held in the United States. Romania's soccer teams have continued to work hard. Today, many Romanian soccer players play on Italian, Spanish, English and Dutch teams.

Below: In 1981, Romania's national soccer team played against the English team at Wembley Stadium in London.

Left: Ilie Nastase was a famous Romanian tennis player of the 1970s. He was the world's number one tennis player two years in a row, in 1972 and 1973. He went on to win more than one hundred other professional titles in his tennis career.

Other Popular Sports

Besides soccer, many Romanians also enjoy playing tennis, running, hiking, cycling, skiing, sailing and swimming.

Many Romanian athletes have won sports competitions all over the world. In 1976, Nadia Comăneci, a Romanian gymnast, became the first person in the world to get a perfect score during the Olympics. In the 2004 Olympics, the country earned eight gold medals in rowing, gymnastics and swimming.

Festivals of the Seasons

Romanians celebrate many religious festivals and festivals that mark the four seasons. *Drăgaica* is a festival that celebrates the summer harvest. In winter, people celebrate *Sorcova* on New Year's Eve. Children brush bunches of twigs over the heads of adults for good luck. The children usually get sweets, cakes or money in return. One spring tradition is for a young man to give the woman he loves a red and white **amulet**.

Easter Traditions

Romania's Easter traditions are quite different from those in other countries. Romanian Easter eggs are **etched** with a *condei*, a sharp tool that looks like a pen. Some popular patterns include flowers and crosses. Red, blue, green and yellow are favourite colours for eggs. Easter breads are popular in Romania. They are shaped like crosses or knots and often have fillings.

Below: These colourfully painted Easter eggs are a Romanian specialty.

Food

Most Romanian food is very flavourful. Preparing the food sometimes takes a long time because Romanian dishes often include many ingredients, such as meat, vegetables, herbs and spices.

Most Romanians eat three meals a day. The main meal of the day is lunch. It usually begins with crusty bread and a bowl of sour soup. Servings of meat and potatoes or fish and salad are also eaten. Lunch often ends with dessert.

Left: In Romania, most meals begin with a small glass of *tuică*. The drink is made from plums.

Left:
A lunch of grilled fish is common for Romanians living near the Black Sea or the Danube River.

Sarmale is a favourite dish in Romania. It is a mixture of rice, chopped meat, onions and spices. The mixture is wrapped in cabbage leaves and cooked in tomato sauce. Another favourite dish is *mititei* or grilled sausages. Different kinds of mititei are made in different regions of the country. Most Romanians also love soup, including turkey soup made with vegetables, rice, lemon juice, parsley and dill, a kind of herb.

A   **B**   **C**   **D**

	National Boundary
	Provincial Boundary
■	Capital City
●	Major Town
	River
▲	Mountain
	Marshland

1

U K R A I N E

2

H U N G A R Y

SATU MARE

MARMURES

SUCEAVA

BOTOSANI

BISTRITA-NASAUD

IASI

MOL

Iași •

SĂLAJ

BIHOR

NEAMT

CLUJ

• Szek

MURES

VASLUI

TRANSYLVANIA

BACĂU

ARAD

HARGHITA

3

ALBA

SIBIU

BRASOV

COVASNA

VRANCEA

GALAȚI

TIMIȘ

HUNEDOARA

Mount Moldoveanu
(2,544 metres)

• Brașov

Southern Carpathians
(Transylvanian Alps)

BUZĂU

BRĂILA

CARAS-SEVERIN

GORJ

VÎLCEA

ARGES

DIMBOVITA

PRAHOVA

IALOMITA

4

MEHEDINTI

OLT

WALACHIA

ILFOV

■ BUCHAREST

CĂLĂRAȘI

DOR

Danube

SERBIA AND MONTENEGRO

DOLJ

TELEORMAN

GIURGIU

Danube

5

B U L G A R I A

ROMANIA

Eastern Carpathians

Western Carpathians

MOLDAVIA

Danube

E

DOVA

UKRAINE

Danube Delta

TULCEA

Lake Razelm

CONSTANȚA
• Constanța

B L A C K
S E A

Alba (county) B3–B4
Arad (county) A2–B3

Bacău (county) C2–D3
Bihor (county) A2–B3
Black Sea D5–E3
Botoșani (county)
C2–D2
Brăila (county) D3–D4
Brașov C3
Brașov (county) C3
Bulgaria B4–E5
Bucharest C4–D4
Buzău (county) C3–D4

Călărași (county) D4
Caraș-Severin
(county) A3–B4
Cluj (county) B2–B3
Constanța E4
Constanța (county)
D4–E5
Covasna (county)
C3–D3

Danube (river) A3–E4
Danube Delta E3–E4
Dimbovita (county)
C3–C4
Dobruja D3–E4
Dolj (county) B4–C5

Eastern Carpathians
C2–C3

Galați (county) D3
Giurgiu (county)
C5–D4
Gorj (county) B3–B4

Harghita (county)
C2–D3
Hunedoara (county)
B3
Hungary A1–A3

Ialomita (county) D4
Iași D2
Iași (county) D2
Ilfov (county) C4–D4

Lake Razelm E4

Above: These children are dressed in traditional Romanian costumes.

Marmureș (county)
B2–C2
Mehedinti (county)
B4
Moldavia D1–D3
Moldova D1–E3
Mount
Moldoveanu C3
Mureș (county) B3–C2

Neamț (county) C2–D2

Olt (county) B4–C5

Prahova (county)
C3–D4

Satu Mare (county)
B2
Serbia and
Montenegro
A3–B5
Sibiu (county) B3–C3

Southern
Carpathians
B3–C3
Suceava (county)
C2–D2
Szek B2

Teleorman (county)
C4–C5
Timiș (county) A3–B3
Transylvania B3–C3
Transylvanian Alps
B3–C3
Tulcea (county) D3–E4

Ukraine B1–E3

Vaslui (county) D2–D3
Vrancea (county) D3

Walachia B4–D4
Western Carpathians
B2–B3

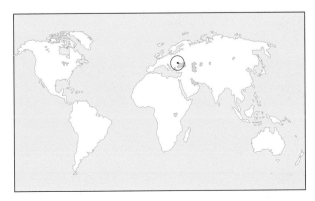

Quick Facts

Official name	Romania
Capital	Bucharest
Official Language	Romanian
Population	22,355,551 (July 2004 estimate)
Land Area	237,500 square kilometres
Counties	Alba, Arad, Argeş, Bacău, Bihor, Bistriţa-Năsaud, Botoşani, Brăila, Braşov, Bucharest (municipality), Buzău, Călăraşi, Caraş-Severin, Cluj, Constanţa, Covasna, Dîmboviţa, Dolj, Galaţi, Giurgiu, Gorj, Harghita, Hunedoara, Ialomita, Iaşi, Ilfov, Maramureş, Mehedinti, Mureş, Neamţ, Olt, Prahova, Sălaj, Satu Mare, Sibiu, Suceava, Teleorman, Timiş, Tulcea, Vaslui, Vîlcea, Vrancea.
Highest Point	Mount Moldoveanu (2,544 metres)
Ethnic Groups	Romanians, Hungarians, Roma, Germans, Ukrainians
Main Religion	Romanian Orthodox Christianity
Major Festivals	Spring Amulet, Drăguica, Sorcova, Easter, Christmas
Currency	Leu (61,645 Romanian Leu = £1 as of July 2004)

Opposite: This beautiful building is the Putna Monastery in Suceava County.

Glossary

amulet: a small charm that is believed to bring good luck or protect against evil.

ancestors: family members from the past, further back than grandparents.

Baroque: a style of the 1600s and 1700s that used fancy, flowery designs.

communist: related to a government that owns all property in the country.

conquered: attacked and took over.

constitution: a set of laws for a country that tells what rights citizens have.

democratic: relating to a government in which citizens can elect their leaders.

embroidered: decorated a piece of cloth or clothes with fancy sewing.

etched: scratched a design into the surface of an object.

ethnic: related to a race or a culture that has similar customs and languages.

exports (n): products sent out of a country to be sold in another country.

fables: fiction stories that teach lessons.

invasions: acts of groups who enter a region to take land or valuables.

mineral springs: springs that are soaked with chemicals from the ground.

monasteries: houses for religious people such as monks or priests.

mosque: a house of worship for those who follow Islam.

municipality: a big city area that has some power to govern itself.

negotiate: to talk to others to decide on a deal or to make a decision.

plateaus: wide, flat areas of land that are surrounded by lower land.

principalities: lands ruled by princes.

privatising: changing from government ownership of industries to ownership by private businesses or individuals.

republic: a country in which citizens elect their own lawmakers.

rural: related to the countryside.

satires: stories that make fun of a particular problem or subject.

uprisings: acts of violence by citizens to fight against a government's rules.

urban: related to cities and large towns.

vocational: related to an occupation, profession or skilled trade.

workforce: the people in a country who work, most often outside the home.

More Books to Read

Black Sea. Wonders of the World series. Corinne J. Naden,
    Rose Blue (Cherrytree Books)

Checkmate in the Carpathians (Passport to Danger).
    Mary Reeves Bell (Bethany House Publishers)

Continents: Europe. L Foster (Heinemann Library)

I come from Romania. Anita Ganeri (Franklin Watts)

Web Sites

www.academickids.com/world/geos/ro.html

www.ici.ro/romania/

www.romaniatourism.com/album.html

www.visiteurope.com/Romania/

Due to the dynamic nature of the Internet, some web sites stay current longer than
others. To find additional web sites, use a reliable search engine with one or more of
the following keywords to help you locate information about Romania. Keywords:
Bucharest, Carpathian Mountains, Nicolae Ceausescu, Danube, Mount Moldoveanu.

Note to parents and teachers
Every effort has been made by the Publishers to ensure that these web sites are
suitable for children; that they are of the highest educational value, and that they
contain no inappropriate or offensive material. However, because of the nature of
the Internet, it is impossible to guarantee that the contents of these sites will not be
altered. We strongly advise that Internet access iş supervised by a responsible adult.

Index